Write Your Story

A Guided Journal for Healing Trauma

Amy Joy, BSW, MPA

Amy Joy is a public speaker, author, and professor. She has dedicated her life to helping those adversely impacted by childhood abuse and trauma. Amy's own experience and work with survivors of sex trafficking, childhood abuse, and those diagnosed with mental illness adds to her education in social work, nonprofit administration, and psychology. To contact Amy Joy for a speaking engagement, please send inquiries to amyjoypresents@gmail.com.

Copyright @ 2021 KDP, Amazon Publishing

All rights reserved

Amy Joy, BSW, MPA

"There is no greater agony than bearing an untold story inside you." ~ Maya Angelo ~

Author's Note

Welcome to a journey of healing through purposeful writing. This style of writing taps into the emotional centers of the brain and helps you create and develop your story. The ability to communicate the things that have happened to us is how the healing process flourishes. The next six weeks are not set in stone. Feel free to jump around or repeat prompts. Through this guided journey, you will have access to the tools you need to continue expressive writing far beyond this program.

Table of Contents

Page 7	"Writing with Purpose"
Page 12	"How to Begin"
Page 14	Week 1
Page 48	Week 2
Page 85	Week 3
Page 120	Week 4
Page 155	Week 5
Page 190	Week 6
Page 226	"Alternative Writing Styles & Programs"
Page 228	References

Writing with Purpose

The practice of writing with emotional expression and intention is *purposeful writing*. It requires a degree of openness to let emotions rise and be known, as well as a degree of awareness to put what you are feeling on the page. This type of writing does not generally come naturally, the aid of prompts is helpful. For those who have quite a bit of buried trauma, emotions, and are unaware of what may lurk beneath the surface, this type of writing can quickly become an emotional rollercoaster. Have some self-care practices at the ready.

Who benefits from purposeful writing?

Everyone, regardless of education, writing style, or ability can benefit from implementing purposeful writing practice. Studies have found there is no difference in the level of benefit between those with higher education and those who had no concept of grammar, syntax, or spelling (Maroney, 2020; Pennebaker, 2013). This type of writing program is not graded or judged; it holds no value outside of the value it brings to the writer. Many who were harshly graded or judged for the writing they produced as a child find a level of freedom when participating in a purposeful writing program. Purposeful writing also goes by the name of expressive writing and autobiographical journaling. Whatever you decide to call it, the purpose is to dig deep and unlock your story.

Releasing Trauma

Writing for deep healing is brave, and for some, the trauma is fresh and raw. For others, the trauma may be deep within the unconscious and planted there in childhood. It does not matter when the events occurred, it just matters that they are being brought to the front of one's awareness and attention and being laid out on paper. The benefits of purposeful writing for all individuals with trauma whether in the past or present can be profound and life-changing (Pennebaker, 2013; Seigel, 2011). The first few weeks of this program may unearth some seriously painful events, thoughts, feelings, and behaviors. It is vital to have a self-care plan in place.

First things first, you may find it helpful to meet with a trusted person to process any negative thinking or behavior (Seigel, 2011; van der Kolk, 2003). It is perfectly normal and acceptable that emotions will rise, recognize them, honor them, and talk about them. Adding additional expressive therapies can be extremely helpful, as they also help reduce negative symptoms of depression and anxiety; and increase self-awareness and brain-body balance.

Find a safe place

Those who write are not necessarily better off reading what they wrote to someone else, or to a group (Pennebaker & Smyth, 2016). This can be beneficial for those who have a trusted person to process that information but if you find yourself not wanting to read what you have written, or share it, DON'T. Some found they are sadder and more depressed when they shared what they had written with a support group. Do not demand that people reveal their writing, respect their boundaries while opening enough emotional space to disclose if they desire to share. Creating a safe, nonjudgmental space is key for group work, but no one needs to tell their story if they are not internally motivated to do so. If you need to, destroy your writings, shred them or bury them, no need to share what you don't want to share.

Setting

When sitting down to write, or if you're an oddball like me, standing to write, be sure it is comfortable, for YOU! Some people love the buzz of people and a coffee shop or bookstore. For others, writing in bed is best. And yet, others write standing at the kitchen counter with a box propping up their computer at eye-level, this technique saves my posture. Yep, that's my preferred way to write. Different types of writing may require a different location and atmosphere. I prefer to write more serious, emotional text in privacy while writing technical or educational material in the buzz of a community.

Types of writing styles

Pay attention to the rhythm of writing, whether freehand or typing, there is a rhythm and flows from the whole body. Pay attention to your breath, your body movements, and your posture. Notice any tension in the body and if there is, release it with the next breath. Movement and rhythm calm the primal centers of the brain, the diencephalon, and the brainstem (Lucero, 2018). Intervention and prevention measures, like purposeful writing, yoga, art, dance, and theatre have a way of creating a balance between brain and body (Perrymam, Blisard, & Moss, 2019; Siegel, 2011). The act of expression pulls implicit, unconscious memory and emotional trauma from the right side of the brain and when in a safe environment, integrate that information into the left side (Lucero, 2018; Siegel, 2011). This action through the corpus callosum, helps us create a narrative of our trauma. It gives a voice to our experience. When we can write, say it, communicate it, we can heal from it.

Before you begin

Recognize that you too, like all human beings, have emotions. They will come up when you begin to write, simply notice them without judgment and move on. There is no need to label your emotions are good or bad, they are what they are, there is no more.

Purposeful writing allows you to create your own story. Where your life began, where you are now, and everything in-between is open for discovery. One of the biggest challenges when writing to heal is finding a way to put the pieces of trauma together in a linear narrative (Loewenstein, 2018). Trauma gets encoded in the brain differently than all other memories, much of it left in an unconscious form. Expressive-purposeful writing draws these pieces out and over time, your story will emerge. Keep in mind, no one has a perfect memory, and whatever perceptions and recall you have is valid. Try not to analyze everything that emerges from your writing, simply notice it at first, and let it come together in its own way and time.

All memory is narrowly viewed by the one experiencing it, telling it, writing about it. Try writing from someone else's perspective. There will be a prompt or two that reminds you of this technique. It provides perspective from another's point of view, and personal insight on any meaning you may assign to the person or event.

You do not need to be a seasoned writer, a professor of English Literature, or a scholar of any type to begin writing (Maroney, 2020; Pennebaker, 2013). You are you, and you will write like you, not Faulkner, Shakespeare, or Stephen King. Just write. Don't compare yourself to other writers, this is for you and you alone. If you choose to write for a career or hobby and share it with the world, great! But that is not the goal and purpose of writing to heal from trauma.

Choosing to write longhand or by typing is totally up to you. There is no significant difference between the two when it comes to the benefits of purposeful writing (Brewin & Lennard, 1999). When I am feeling introspective, I find it helpful to write longhand, it allows me to slow down. Typing, on the other hand, allows me to write quickly. Whatever technique you use, find your rhythm. Try using *stream of consciousness*, writing without stopping, whether writing longhand and typing (Cameron, 2014).

Challenges or Concerns When Writing

There is a concern and firmly held belief by many that those who have experienced trauma are fragile flowers on the brink of destruction. This is rarely the case. The fact that those who have experienced trauma are willing to write about themselves and their experiences speaks to their resilience (Siegel, 2011). The analogy of people who have experienced trauma as broken into pieces is a myth. Instead, think of each event and difficult experience as a strong cinderblock that has built a beautiful and strong castle. Trauma is not the end, it can be and often is, a foundation for strength and fortitude.

With every writing prompt, whether you are doing this on your own, in a group, or implementing this program in your agency or organization, have a rule that any writing prompt may be skipped if the participant feels it will be too much for them. Yes, people are resilient, but we also do not want to push before someone is ready to process a particular topic. Feel free to jump around and create your program with the prompts as you see fit.

A little obsessed

For some, implementing a new routine or program can fuel obsessive tendencies (Pennebaker, 2013). Fifteen minutes of writing a day may turn into eighty, and then four hours, and before you know it, writing has become a full-time job that doesn't pay the bills. If you are one of these left-brainy types, take it easy, create a plan for balance and stick to it. That can be easier said than done, I know, I am a left-brainy type and have turned my obsession into a profession. However, this is not for everyone. Recognize your tendencies and adjust accordingly.

But what if someone reads it?

A deeply personal issue for many of us is having someone in our past, or maybe in the present, who has discovered our writing and used it against us. When I was twelve-years-old, I wrote in a journal about things happening at home. The person who found it was also the person who was abusing me, it did not go well. This is the case for many survivors of child abuse. It is perfectly okay and acceptable to hide or destroy your writing. The act of writing is the most important part of healing, not keeping it.

Relationship changes

We were created and designed to have close relationships with other people (Cronin et al., 2014). This is just a biological function of survival for all pack animals. Simply put, we need people, and they need us. Working through this writing program may change the dynamics of your relationships. You may recognize some toxic traits, co-dependency, or even abuse within your relationships. Not everyone will be a fan of your newly found insight and positive life changes. You may get a new job, want to relocate to a safer community or separate from those who hurt you. What you do with these relationships is up to you but whatever you choose, find positive support to include in your circle of friends. You may find this support at church, in a smaller community group, or maybe a club. Seek out the ones who will support you through this process.

How to Begin

Not all trauma is in our awareness, leave it alone if it does not bother you, or come up in a way that you cannot deal with it in a safe place and with a safe person (Pennebaker, 2013). Many people have histories of childhood trauma but not all trauma needs to be dealt with, or at least at any given moment in time. Let the writing lead you where it needs to go, poking and prodding at issues that are not problems in your life will side-track your progress. It is a distraction, just go with the flow. Begin your writing with what is bothering you right now.

Create a Schedule

Begin with five days in mind (Pennebaker, 2013). Give this program five consecutive days before chucking it off a cliff. Set aside at least fifteen minutes a day, find a comfortable place, and write. Julia Cameron, author of The Artist's Way suggests starting each day with what she calls "morning pages." Cameron writes three pages, longhand, every morning. Her writing is not always profound and life-altering, but it provides a routine for writing, and this is very important. If you cannot carve out some time in the morning, ask yourself when you do have downtime during your day. If you do not have any downtime in your day, something in your schedule needs to change, not just for the sake of purposeful writing, but for overall balance in your daily life.

Some basic steps

- Write for at least five days each week, for the next six weeks.
- Find a unique place to write, a place just for you and conducive for energy flow.

- Use different tools to find your favorite. Try writing longhand and typing. Try out different pens, pencils, paper, notebook, laptop, iPad, or computer. Your preferences will be unique to you.
- Allow yourself to hide or destroy what you write. This may provide the comfort and protection needed to write with intention.
- Allow yourself to skip a difficult prompt. You do not have to stick to the prompts in order, if something is too difficult or you need to write about something else for the day, change it up.
- Using a *stream of consciousness*, write for at least fifteen consecutive minutes. Don't think, don't stop.
- Keep it simple. Find your spot, pick a time, follow the prompts, write your story.
- Try "Morning Pages." Write 3 pages, longhand, every morning (Cameron, 2020).
- Keep a separate journal. This journal is a dandy tool but if you are afraid of someone finding your writing or you would like to share this book with someone, a separate journal can solve a lot of potential issues.

The first five days

To begin this writing program, we are going to dive into the deep. An exploration into the trauma that has been impacting your life the most is where you will begin. Write consistently for at least fifteen minutes, only recalling what happened during the event, how you felt then, and how you feel now.

As you write, ask yourself how this event has impacted your life, your relationships with yourself and others, and in what other ways your life has changed because of this event. Dig deep and allow your emotions to fill the page. Don't stop too long to think, just write. It may be helpful to write out the questions you would like answers to, ahead of time. Then simply answer those questions.

Week 1

Day 1: Write about a negative or traumatic event that has deeply impacted your life. Be as detailed as possible. What did you see, hear, taste, smell, touch, and feel? Before you write, notice how your body feels. Is there tension? Where in your body? What are your emotions? Are you sad, angry, apathetic, or happy?

After writing the exercise. Answer the following questions.
What sensations do you feel in your body? Has it changed from before you began writing?
What emotions are you experiencing? (Sad, angry, happy, etc.)
What did you find meaningful about today's writing?

_____
_____
_____
_____
_____
_____
_____
_____
_____
_____
_____
_____
_____
_____
_____
_____
_____
_____
_____
_____
_____
_____
_____
_____
_____
_____
_____
_____

Day 2: Write about the same event you wrote about on Day 1, or you may choose a different traumatic event, and really explore your thoughts and feelings. In what specific ways has this event impacted your daily life?

Before you write, notice how your body feels. Is there tension? Where in your body? What are your emotions? Are you sad, angry, apathetic, or happy?

_____
_____
_____
_____
_____
_____
_____
_____
_____
_____
_____
_____
_____
_____
_____
_____
_____
_____
_____
_____
_____
_____
_____

After writing the exercise. Answer the following questions.
What sensations do you feel in your body? Has it changed from before you began writing?
What emotions are you experiencing? (Sad, angry, happy, etc.)
What did you find meaningful about today's writing?

_____
_____
_____
_____
_____
_____
_____
_____
_____
_____
_____
_____
_____
_____
_____
_____
_____
_____
_____
_____
_____
_____
_____

Day 3: Choose an event in your early childhood, before the age of 12, that deeply impacted your life. Examine how this event changed you. Dig deep to discover your feelings about this event and write. Be sure to take a quick assessment of your body and emotional state.

Before you write, notice how your body feels. Is there tension? Where in your body? What are your emotions? Are you sad, angry, apathetic, or happy?

_____
_____
_____
_____
_____
_____
_____
_____
_____
_____
_____
_____
_____
_____
_____
_____
_____
_____
_____
_____
_____
_____
_____
_____

After writing the exercise. Answer the following questions.
What sensations do you feel in your body? Has it changed from before you began writing?
What emotions are you experiencing? (Sad, angry, happy, etc.)
What did you find meaningful about today's writing?

_____
_____
_____
_____
_____
_____
_____
_____
_____
_____
_____
_____
_____
_____
_____
_____
_____
_____
_____
_____
_____
_____

Day 4: Use the event you came up with on Day 3 and explore deeper into your feelings about this event. How has it impacted your life and relationships? How might your life be different if this event had not occurred?

Before you write, notice how your body feels. Is there tension? Where in your body? What are your emotions? Are you sad, angry, apathetic, or happy?

_____
_____
_____
_____
_____
_____
_____
_____
_____
_____
_____
_____
_____
_____
_____
_____
_____
_____
_____
_____
_____
_____
_____
_____
_____

After writing the exercise. Answer the following questions.
What sensations do you feel in your body? Has it changed from before you began writing?
What emotions are you experiencing? (Sad, angry, happy, etc.)
What did you find meaningful about today's writing?

_____
_____
_____
_____
_____
_____
_____
_____
_____
_____
_____
_____
_____
_____
_____
_____
_____
_____
_____
_____
_____
_____
_____
_____
_____
_____
_____
_____

Day 5: Today is the last day of the first week. Review the first four days of purposeful writing and see if you can find any themes. Does sadness or anger creep into your writing? Do you find yourself feeling more emotional about one event over another? Why might that be? What have you learned about yourself so far?
Before you write, notice how your body feels. Is there tension? Where in your body? What are your emotions? Are you sad, angry, apathetic, or happy?

_____
_____
_____
_____
_____
_____
_____
_____
_____
_____
_____
_____
_____
_____
_____
_____
_____
_____
_____
_____
_____
_____
_____
_____

After writing the exercise. Answer the following questions.
What sensations do you feel in your body? Has it changed from before you began writing?
What emotions are you experiencing? (Sad, angry, happy, etc.)
What did you find meaningful about today's writing?

_____
_____
_____
_____
_____
_____
_____
_____
_____
_____
_____
_____
_____
_____
_____
_____
_____
_____
_____
_____
_____
_____
_____
_____
_____
_____

End of Week Assessment

Have you noticed any changes in your mood, eating habits, sleep changes, drug or alcohol use, pain in your body, or anything else you can notice? Take ten minutes and review your experience over this first week.

Are you sleeping better, or falling asleep faster?
Are you eating a balanced diet? Not over or under eating?
Are you happier, sadder, angrier, or less emotional overall?
Are you using fewer drugs or alcohol?
Have you noticed any changes in your close relationships?

_____
_____
_____
_____
_____
_____
_____
_____
_____
_____
_____
_____
_____
_____
_____
_____
_____
_____
_____
_____

Week 2

In Week 2, we will explore what it means to see things from someone else's perspective. This week is all about insight and perspective. Try using each prompt as an opportunity to flip the script and see things from the other side. Really explore what thoughts and feelings you think some else is thinking and feeling about an event you have experienced.

Day 1

Think back on the past week and choose an event, negative or positive, that impacted your life in some way. Use this event to explore what someone else who also experienced this event with you may have thought or felt about it. Describe the event, how you felt and thought about it, and then describe the event from the perspective of someone else who experienced this event with you. Before you write, notice how your body feels. Is there tension? Where in your body? What are your emotions? Are you sad, angry, apathetic, or happy?

_____
_____
_____
_____
_____
_____
_____
_____
_____
_____
_____
_____
_____
_____
_____

After writing the exercise. Answer the following questions.
What sensations do you feel in your body? Has it changed from before you began writing?
What emotions are you experiencing? (Sad, angry, happy, etc.)
What did you find meaningful about today's writing?

_____
_____
_____
_____
_____
_____
_____
_____
_____
_____
_____
_____
_____
_____
_____
_____
_____
_____
_____
_____
_____
_____
_____
_____
_____
_____
_____
_____
_____

Day 2: You can choose the same event from Week 2, Day 1, or a different event, now write it from the perspective of an outsider. An outsider would a nonjudgmental observer. Use your imagination. This nonbiased observer may not have been present at the event, just pretend, and then write from their perspective. What may they say about the event, your reaction to the event, or how others felt about it?

Before you write, notice how your body feels. Is there tension? Where in your body? What are your emotions? Are you sad, angry, apathetic, or happy?

_____
_____
_____
_____
_____
_____
_____
_____
_____
_____
_____
_____
_____
_____
_____
_____
_____
_____
_____
_____
_____
_____
_____
_____

After writing the exercise. Answer the following questions.
What sensations do you feel in your body? Has it changed from before you began writing?
What emotions are you experiencing? (Sad, angry, happy, etc.)
What did you find meaningful about today's writing?

_____
_____
_____
_____
_____
_____
_____
_____
_____
_____
_____
_____
_____
_____
_____
_____
_____
_____
_____
_____
_____
_____
_____
_____
_____
_____
_____

Day 3: Today, use your imagination even further, choose a story you have heard in the news or social media. Describe the event and the people involved. How do you think they may have felt or thought about what happened? What was important or meaningful about the event? What resonated with you about the story? Why? Before you write, notice how your body feels. Is there tension? Where in your body? What are your emotions? Are you sad, angry, apathetic, or happy?

_____
_____
_____
_____
_____
_____
_____
_____
_____
_____
_____
_____
_____
_____
_____
_____
_____
_____
_____
_____
_____
_____
_____
_____
_____
_____

After writing the exercise. Answer the following questions.
What sensations do you feel in your body? Has it changed from before you began writing?
What emotions are you experiencing? (Sad, angry, happy, etc.)
What did you find meaningful about today's writing?

Day 4: Choose an event from your past, one in which someone else reacted badly. Describe the event. Why do you think the other person behaved the way they did? Is there something in their past that may have led to their reaction? How did you respond to their behavior? What do you suppose they were thinking and feeling? What were you thinking and feeling? Were there similarities in your reaction to the event? If so, what were they?

Before you write, notice how your body feels. Is there tension? Where in your body? What are your emotions? Are you sad, angry, apathetic, or happy?

After writing the exercise. Answer the following questions.
What sensations do you feel in your body? Has it changed from before you began writing?
What emotions are you experiencing? (Sad, angry, happy, etc.)
What did you find meaningful about today's writing?

_____
_____
_____
_____
_____
_____
_____
_____
_____
_____
_____
_____
_____
_____
_____
_____
_____
_____
_____
_____
_____
_____
_____
_____
_____
_____

Day 5: Thinking back on this week's writing, what resonated with you the most? Did you learn something important about yourself or someone else? Describe your experience of this week's writing assignments.

Before you write, notice how your body feels. Is there tension? Where in your body? What are your emotions? Are you sad, angry, apathetic, or happy?

___

After writing the exercise. Answer the following questions.
What sensations do you feel in your body? Has it changed from before you began writing?
What emotions are you experiencing? (Sad, angry, happy, etc.)
What did you find meaningful about today's writing?

_____
_____
_____
_____
_____
_____
_____
_____
_____
_____
_____
_____
_____
_____
_____
_____
_____
_____
_____
_____
_____
_____
_____
_____
_____
_____
_____

End of Week Assessment

Have you noticed any changes in your mood, eating habits, sleep changes, drug or alcohol use, pain in your body, or anything else you can notice? Take ten minutes and review your experience over this first week.
Are you sleeping better, or falling asleep faster?
Are you eating a balanced diet? Not over or under eating?
Are you happier, sadder, angrier, or less emotional overall?
Are you using fewer drugs or alcohol?
Have you noticed any changes in your close relationships?

_____
_____
_____
_____
_____
_____
_____
_____
_____
_____
_____
_____
_____
_____
_____
_____
_____
_____
_____
_____

Week 3

This week is all about practicing different types of writing styles. We begin with *stream of consciousness*, writing without stopping for a set amount of time. For each week, set a timer for ten minutes and just write. We'll end the week with *semiautomatic* writing. This is stream of conscious writing on steroids, or tranquilizers, depending on your perspective. *Semiautomatic* writing is writing with no conscious or linear thought. Not everyone likes this kind of writing, but it can be highly effective for revealing deep emotions and issues.

To conduct *semiautomatic* writing, place a towel or washcloth over your hand as you write and just let go. If you are writing on a laptop or computer, pick a spot on the wall or in the room and focus on that as you type. Close your eyes if that helps. Some people describe this type of writing as trance-like, just give it a try, if you don't like it, go back to *stream of consciousness*.

Day 1: Use today to practice *stream of consciousness* writing. Choose any topic and write without thinking, without stopping, just write. You can shorten the time to ten minutes. The only rule is, do not stop writing until the timer goes off.

Before you write, notice how your body feels. Is there tension? Where in your body? What are your emotions? Are you sad, angry, apathetic, or happy?

_____
_____
_____
_____
_____
_____
_____

After writing the exercise. Answer the following questions.
What sensations do you feel in your body? Has it changed from before you began writing?
What emotions are you experiencing? (Sad, angry, happy, etc.)
What did you find meaningful about today's writing?

_____
_____
_____
_____
_____
_____
_____
_____
_____
_____
_____
_____
_____
_____
_____
_____
_____
_____
_____
_____
_____
_____
_____
_____
_____
_____

Day 2: Today, practice writing with *stream of consciousness* once more. This time, notice what is around you. What do you feel, hear, smell, and see? Ten minutes, go!

Before you write, notice how your body feels. Is there tension? Where in your body? What are your emotions? Are you sad, angry, apathetic, or happy?

___

After writing the exercise. Answer the following questions.
What sensations do you feel in your body? Has it changed from before you began writing?
What emotions are you experiencing? (Sad, angry, happy, etc.)
What did you find meaningful about today's writing?

Day 3: Today, we will practice *semiautomatic* writing. Close your eyes or place a towel or washcloth over your hand as you write, set the timer for ten minutes, and write. Do not think, do not stop, just move your hand, and let it flow. Choose an event from your past, negative or positive, and just write.

Before you write, notice how your body feels. Is there tension? Where in your body? What are your emotions? Are you sad, angry, apathetic, or happy?

_____
_____
_____
_____
_____
_____
_____
_____
_____
_____
_____
_____
_____
_____
_____
_____
_____
_____
_____
_____
_____
_____
_____
_____
_____
_____

After writing the exercise. Answer the following questions.
What sensations do you feel in your body? Has it changed from before you began writing?
What emotions are you experiencing? (Sad, angry, happy, etc.)
What did you find meaningful about today's writing?

_____
_____
_____
_____
_____
_____
_____
_____
_____
_____
_____
_____
_____
_____
_____
_____
_____
_____
_____
_____
_____
_____
_____
_____
_____
_____

Day 4: Once more, practice *semiautomatic* writing. If the previous exercise resulted in a jumble of words, no worries, that happens sometimes. Try it once more. Choose an event from your past, negative or positive, set the timer for ten minutes, and write. Before you write, notice how your body feels. Is there tension? Where in your body? What are your emotions? Are you sad, angry, apathetic, or happy?

_____
_____
_____
_____
_____
_____
_____
_____
_____
_____
_____
_____
_____
_____
_____
_____
_____
_____
_____
_____
_____
_____
_____

After writing the exercise. Answer the following questions.
What sensations do you feel in your body? Has it changed from before you began writing?
What emotions are you experiencing? (Sad, angry, happy, etc.)
What did you find meaningful about today's writing?

_____
_____
_____
_____
_____
_____
_____
_____
_____
_____
_____
_____
_____
_____
_____
_____
_____
_____
_____
_____
_____
_____
_____
_____
_____

Day 5: Review the writing you have done this week and describe your experience. Did you like writing with *stream of consciousness* or *semiautomatic*? What did you discover about yourself?
Before you write, notice how your body feels. Is there tension? Where in your body? What are your emotions? Are you sad, angry, apathetic, or happy?

_____
_____
_____
_____
_____
_____
_____
_____
_____
_____
_____
_____
_____
_____
_____
_____
_____
_____
_____
_____
_____
_____
_____
_____

After writing the exercise. Answer the following questions.
What sensations do you feel in your body? Has it changed from before you began writing?
What emotions are you experiencing? (Sad, angry, happy, etc.)
What did you find meaningful about today's writing?

End of Week Assessment

Have you noticed any changes in your mood, eating habits, sleep changes, drug or alcohol use, pain in your body, or anything else you can notice? Take ten minutes and review your experience over this first week.

Are you sleeping better, or falling asleep faster?
Are you eating a balanced diet? Not over or under eating?
Are you happier, sadder, angrier, or less emotional overall?
Are you using fewer drugs or alcohol?
Have you noticed any changes in your close relationships?

_____
_____
_____
_____
_____
_____
_____
_____
_____
_____
_____
_____
_____
_____
_____
_____
_____
_____
_____
_____
_____
_____

Week 4

This week is all about gratitude. To be honest, trauma is rarely a joyful experience. Finding joy in events that are terrifying and life-threatening seems impossible, or at best, impractical. Don't feel compelled to find joy where there isn't any, but if there is any positive in those events, try to pull them out. No need to dive into major traumas, this is to simply give you some practice finding some positive aspects in negative events. Use as many negative words as you like but try to add a few of the positive words listed below.

Love, easy, peaceful, kind, joyful, thankful, proud, gentle, trust, perfect, fun, nice, good, happy, laugh, inspire, courageous, merry, romance, graceful, calm, kind, strong, brave, caring, acceptance, …

Day 1

Using some words that convey joy and thankfulness, choose an event in your past and describe the way you felt then and the way you feel now. You may not have many positive words to use at first but do your best to implement gratitude. Set the timer for ten minutes and write.

Before you write, notice how your body feels. Is there tension? Where in your body? What are your emotions? Are you sad, angry, apathetic, or happy?

_____
_____
_____
_____
_____
_____
_____
_____

After writing the exercise. Answer the following questions.
What sensations do you feel in your body? Has it changed from before you began writing?
What emotions are you experiencing? (Sad, angry, happy, etc.)
What did you find meaningful about today's writing?

Day 2: Review the response to the previous writing prompt and describe your experience using words of gratitude. What did you notice about your experience? Was it difficult to find positive aspects from a difficult event? Did you find yourself resistant to the assignment? Why or why not?

Before you write, notice how your body feels. Is there tension? Where in your body? What are your emotions? Are you sad, angry, apathetic, or happy?

After writing the exercise. Answer the following questions.
What sensations do you feel in your body? Has it changed from before you began writing?
What emotions are you experiencing? (Sad, angry, happy, etc.)
What did you find meaningful about today's writing?

_____
_____
_____
_____
_____
_____
_____
_____
_____
_____
_____
_____
_____
_____
_____
_____
_____
_____
_____
_____
_____
_____
_____
_____
_____
_____
_____
_____
_____
_____

Day 3: Today, we explore forgiveness. Is there someone in your life you have been holding a grudge against? What were the circumstances surrounding the hurt this person created in your life? How did you feel when the event(s) happened? How do you feel now? What would need to happen to forgive this person? Imagine yourself in front of this person, how would the conversation go? Set the timer for 15 minutes and write!

Before you write, notice how your body feels. Is there tension? Where in your body? What are your emotions? Are you sad, angry, apathetic, or happy?

_____
_____
_____
_____
_____
_____
_____
_____
_____
_____
_____
_____
_____
_____
_____
_____
_____
_____
_____
_____
_____
_____
_____
_____
_____

After writing the exercise. Answer the following questions.
What sensations do you feel in your body? Has it changed from before you began writing?
What emotions are you experiencing? (Sad, angry, happy, etc.)
What did you find meaningful about today's writing?

_____
_____
_____
_____
_____
_____
_____
_____
_____
_____
_____
_____
_____
_____
_____
_____
_____
_____
_____
_____
_____
_____
_____
_____
_____
_____
_____

Day 4: Today, choose a difficult event from your past or present. How did this event change your life? Have you developed strengths to overcome the situation? What part of this situation was, or is, positive? What are you grateful for? Was there someone in this situation who you had a difficult time forgiving? Describe the dynamics of the relationship then and now. Set the timer for 15 minutes and go!

Before you write, notice how your body feels. Is there tension? Where in your body? What are your emotions? Are you sad, angry, apathetic, or happy?

After writing the exercise. Answer the following questions.
What sensations do you feel in your body? Has it changed from before you began writing?
What emotions are you experiencing? (Sad, angry, happy, etc.)
What did you find meaningful about today's writing?

_____
_____
_____
_____
_____
_____
_____
_____
_____
_____
_____
_____
_____
_____
_____
_____
_____
_____
_____
_____
_____
_____
_____
_____
_____
_____
_____
_____
_____
_____

Day 5: Review one of your previous writings from this week, what resonated with you the most? Why was this important to you? Were you able to find some gratitude in a negative situation or evaluate some unforgiveness in your life?

Before you write, notice how your body feels. Is there tension? Where in your body? What are your emotions? Are you sad, angry, apathetic, or happy?

___

After writing the exercise. Answer the following questions.
What sensations do you feel in your body? Has it changed from before you began writing?
What emotions are you experiencing? (Sad, angry, happy, etc.)
What did you find meaningful about today's writing?

End of Week Assessment

Have you noticed any changes in your mood, eating habits, sleep changes, drug or alcohol use, pain in your body, or anything else you can notice? Take ten minutes and review your experience over this first week.

Are you sleeping better, or falling asleep faster?
Are you eating a balanced diet? Not over or under eating?
Are you happier, sadder, angrier, or less emotional overall?
Are you using fewer drugs or alcohol?
Have you noticed any changes in your close relationships?

_____
_____
_____
_____
_____
_____
_____
_____
_____
_____
_____
_____
_____
_____
_____
_____
_____
_____
_____
_____
_____
_____

Week 5

This week is all about how to give a voice to your story. A linear and logical narrative is an important piece to healing from trauma. We'll begin with the setting of your traumatic event(s), develop our characters, and describe the details. Give yourself some grace this week. There may be some additional emotional upheaval. Be prepared for some downtime and self-care. This week gives you the structure for creating your story and can be repeated as much as you want.

Day 1

Think about a traumatic event from your past. Describe the event. What was the setting like? Be very specific. What were the events happening in and around the setting? No need to set a time limit, just write until there is nothing more to report about the setting of the event.

Before you write, notice how your body feels. Is there tension? Where in your body? What are your emotions? Are you sad, angry, apathetic, or happy?

_____
_____
_____
_____
_____
_____
_____
_____
_____
_____
_____
_____
_____

After writing the exercise. Answer the following questions.
What sensations do you feel in your body? Has it changed from before you began writing?
What emotions are you experiencing? (Sad, angry, happy, etc.)
What did you find meaningful about today's writing?

_____
_____
_____
_____
_____
_____
_____
_____
_____
_____
_____
_____
_____
_____
_____
_____
_____
_____
_____
_____
_____
_____
_____
_____

Day 2: Thinking about the same event from the previous prompt, briefly describe the event once more, this time giving special attention to the people involved in the experience. What were their thoughts, feelings, and actions before the event? What were your thoughts, feelings, and actions before the event? What was your interaction with the people involved in the event before it occurred?

Before you write, notice how your body feels. Is there tension? Where in your body? What are your emotions? Are you sad, angry, apathetic, or happy?

_____
_____
_____
_____
_____
_____
_____
_____
_____
_____
_____
_____
_____
_____
_____
_____
_____
_____
_____
_____
_____
_____
_____

After writing the exercise. Answer the following questions.
What sensations do you feel in your body? Has it changed from before you began writing?
What emotions are you experiencing? (Sad, angry, happy, etc.)
What did you find meaningful about today's writing?

_____
_____
_____
_____
_____
_____
_____
_____
_____
_____
_____
_____
_____
_____
_____
_____
_____
_____
_____
_____
_____
_____
_____
_____
_____
_____

Day 3: Using the same event from Day 1 & 2, describe the event once more. Pay attention to how the event changed the way you thought, felt, or behaved during the event. What happened to make you react the way you did? What happened that changed the behavior of those around you? Explore the actions of the event as it was happening.

Before you write, notice how your body feels. Is there tension? Where in your body? What are your emotions? Are you sad, angry, apathetic, or happy?

_____
_____
_____
_____
_____
_____
_____
_____
_____
_____
_____
_____
_____
_____
_____
_____
_____
_____
_____
_____
_____
_____
_____
_____

After writing the exercise. Answer the following questions.
What sensations do you feel in your body? Has it changed from before you began writing?
What emotions are you experiencing? (Sad, angry, happy, etc.)
What did you find meaningful about today's writing?

_____
_____
_____
_____
_____
_____
_____
_____
_____
_____
_____
_____
_____
_____
_____
_____
_____
_____
_____
_____
_____
_____
_____
_____
_____
_____

Day 4: Yep, we're still working on the same traumatic event. Today, describe the event in detail from the beginning, describe the people, feelings, thoughts, and behavior. Describe how this event changed your life immediately, and long-term. Did you find anything meaningful arise?

Before you write, notice how your body feels. Is there tension? Where in your body? What are your emotions? Are you sad, angry, apathetic, or happy?

_____
_____
_____
_____
_____
_____
_____
_____
_____
_____
_____
_____
_____
_____
_____
_____
_____
_____
_____
_____
_____
_____
_____
_____
_____
_____
_____

After writing the exercise. Answer the following questions.
What sensations do you feel in your body? Has it changed from before you began writing?
What emotions are you experiencing? (Sad, angry, happy, etc.)
What did you find meaningful about today's writing?

Day 5: Without thinking, simply write the traumatic event you have been working on this week. You have been slowly creating your narrative for this particular event. Write the story from beginning to end. No need to set a time limit.

Before you write, notice how your body feels. Is there tension? Where in your body? What are your emotions? Are you sad, angry, apathetic, or happy?

After writing the exercise. Answer the following questions.
What sensations do you feel in your body? Has it changed from before you began writing?
What emotions are you experiencing? (Sad, angry, happy, etc.)
What did you find meaningful about today's writing?

_____
_____
_____
_____
_____
_____
_____
_____
_____
_____
_____
_____
_____
_____
_____
_____
_____
_____
_____
_____
_____
_____
_____
_____
_____
_____
_____
_____
_____

End of Week Assessment

Have you noticed any changes in your mood, eating habits, sleep changes, drug or alcohol use, pain in your body, or anything else you can notice? Take ten minutes and review your experience over this first week.

Are you sleeping better, or falling asleep faster?
Are you eating a balanced diet? Not over or under eating?
Are you happier, sadder, angrier, or less emotional overall?
Are you using fewer drugs or alcohol?
Have you noticed any changes in your close relationships?

_____
_____
_____
_____
_____
_____
_____
_____
_____
_____
_____
_____
_____
_____
_____
_____
_____
_____
_____
_____
_____
_____
_____
_____

Week 6

This week, we will explore trauma from different perspectives, locations, and writing styles.

Day 1: Find a new place to write. Go to a new coffee shop, choose to sit outside, or in a different room to get your writing done today. A location change can activate different parts of your brain and notice new things. Describe your new setting. How does it smell, look, and feel? While in this new setting, describe whatever event that comes up. Is there something in your new setting that reminds you of the event?
Before you write, notice how your body feels. Is there tension? Where in your body? What are your emotions? Are you sad, angry, apathetic, or happy?

_____
_____
_____
_____
_____
_____
_____
_____
_____
_____
_____
_____
_____
_____
_____
_____
_____
_____

After writing the exercise. Answer the following questions.
What sensations do you feel in your body? Has it changed from before you began writing?
What emotions are you experiencing? (Sad, angry, happy, etc.)
What did you find meaningful about today's writing?

_____
_____
_____
_____
_____
_____
_____
_____
_____
_____
_____
_____
_____
_____
_____
_____
_____
_____
_____
_____
_____
_____
_____
_____
_____
_____
_____

Day 2: Write in front of a mirror. Find a relatively large mirror and stare at your reflection. This can be difficult for some people, particularly those who have dysmorphia and severe dissociative disorders. It can be distressing but do your best to look at yourself and view yourself as others view you. Describe your emotions related to how you view yourself and how you perceive others perceive you. Set the timer for ten minutes and write!

Before you write, notice how your body feels. Is there tension? Where in your body? What are your emotions? Are you sad, angry, apathetic, or happy?

_____
_____
_____
_____
_____
_____
_____
_____
_____
_____
_____
_____
_____
_____
_____
_____
_____
_____
_____
_____
_____
_____
_____
_____

After writing the exercise. Answer the following questions.
What sensations do you feel in your body? Has it changed from before you began writing?
What emotions are you experiencing? (Sad, angry, happy, etc.)
What did you find meaningful about today's writing?

_____
_____
_____
_____
_____
_____
_____
_____
_____
_____
_____
_____
_____
_____
_____
_____
_____
_____
_____
_____
_____
_____
_____
_____
_____
_____
_____
_____

Day 3: Find a place to write where you feel especially safe and peaceful. For some, this is outdoors, a library, or a bedroom. Describe your surroundings and explain why you feel secure in this place. What places have you been that you do not feel safe? Why? Are there any other places where you do feel secure? Where are they?

Before you write, notice how your body feels. Is there tension? Where in your body? What are your emotions? Are you sad, angry, apathetic, or happy?

_____
_____
_____
_____
_____
_____
_____
_____
_____
_____
_____
_____
_____
_____
_____
_____
_____
_____
_____
_____
_____
_____
_____
_____
_____
_____
_____

After writing the exercise. Answer the following questions.
What sensations do you feel in your body? Has it changed from before you began writing?
What emotions are you experiencing? (Sad, angry, happy, etc.)
What did you find meaningful about today's writing?

_____
_____
_____
_____
_____
_____
_____
_____
_____
_____
_____
_____
_____
_____
_____
_____
_____
_____
_____
_____
_____
_____
_____
_____
_____
_____
_____
_____

Day 4: For 20 minutes write about a traumatic experience with the aid of symbols from the past. You may experience flooding or flashbacks, and if these become too painful, come back to this exercise at a later date. Utilize symbols like filling a room with a scent, location (basement, bathroom, or car), clothing, or pictures that remind you of the event. Spend some time feeling, thinking, and experiencing the items or surroundings. Use *stream of consciousness*, try not to think, set the timer for 20 minutes, and write.

Before you write, notice how your body feels. Is there tension? Where in your body? What are your emotions? Are you sad, angry, apathetic, or happy?

_____
_____
_____
_____
_____
_____
_____
_____
_____
_____
_____
_____
_____
_____
_____
_____
_____
_____
_____
_____
_____
_____

After writing the exercise. Answer the following questions.
What sensations do you feel in your body? Has it changed from before you began writing?
What emotions are you experiencing? (Sad, angry, happy, etc.)
What did you find meaningful about today's writing?

_____
_____
_____
_____
_____
_____
_____
_____
_____
_____
_____
_____
_____
_____
_____
_____
_____
_____
_____
_____
_____
_____
_____
_____
_____
_____
_____
_____

Day 5: Today, we'll explore how to write an imaginative story. Take some time and imagine what your life would have been without traumatic events in your life. How would your life be different? How would your life be the same? What are some things you love about the life you have? What are some elements of your life you would choose to change? Examine what type of place you would live, the job or career you would have, the car you would drive, and the relationships you would have.

Before you write, notice how your body feels. Is there tension? Where in your body? What are your emotions? Are you sad, angry, apathetic, or happy?

_____
_____
_____
_____
_____
_____
_____
_____
_____
_____
_____
_____
_____
_____
_____
_____
_____
_____
_____
_____
_____
_____
_____
_____

After writing the exercise. Answer the following questions.
What sensations do you feel in your body? Has it changed from before you began writing?
What emotions are you experiencing? (Sad, angry, happy, etc.)
What did you find meaningful about today's writing?

_____
_____
_____
_____
_____
_____
_____
_____
_____
_____
_____
_____
_____
_____
_____
_____
_____
_____
_____
_____
_____
_____
_____
_____
_____
_____
_____

End of Program Assessment

Have you noticed any changes in your mood, eating habits, sleep changes, drug or alcohol use, pain in your body, or anything else you can notice? Take ten minutes and review your experience over this first week.

Are you sleeping better, or falling asleep faster?
Are you eating a balanced diet? Not over or under eating?
Are you happier, sadder, angrier, or less emotional overall?
Are you using fewer drugs or alcohol?
Have you noticed any changes in your close relationships?

_____
_____
_____
_____
_____
_____
_____
_____
_____
_____
_____
_____
_____
_____
_____
_____
_____
_____
_____
_____
_____
_____

Alternative Writing Styles & Programs

Some may love the structure and comprehensive assessments through this guided journal, but for others, a simpler approach may be useful. Children, ages 5 to 17, often cannot recall and reflect on past events in the way adults can. A program called the *Imagine Project* is a simple writing tool for children (Maroney, 2020). The writing prompts can be adjusted, depending upon age and development. Seven simple steps are involved in the program and can be repeated as many times as desired.

1. Gratitude. Select up to three things you love about your life and write for ten minutes.

2. Reflection. Select up to three things that have been challenging in your life, write for ten minutes.

3. Imagine. Write a story about something challenging in your life. Begin each new sentence with the word, "imagine..."

4. Possibilities. Imagine a story of how your life would be without challenges. Begin each new sentence with "imagine. . ."

5. I am, I can, I will. Turn your imagined dreams into statement sentences using "I am...," "I can...," and "I will..."

6. Do. Write down three things that would turn your dreams into reality.

7. Repeat. For 30 days repeat these steps.

Memoir as Testimony

The experience of trauma often leaves survivors struggling for words (Loewenstein, 2018). The act of telling our trauma stories is essential for healing but without access to language, we fail to release the hurt that keeps us locked away. A study done with survivors of the Holocaust found that through the process of intentional journaling, themes of loneliness, loss, and isolation emerged (Duchin &Wiseman, 2019). After the research was concluded, the 13 participants reported a greater sense of connectedness with self and others, and an understanding of who they were as a result of telling their stories. The ability to create a narrative from our pain is often the insight needed to choose life and joy, every day.

Creating a memoir is no easy task but can be done bit by bit (Goldberg, 2011; Karr, 2015). Writing with intention, emotion, and reflection is courageous. Every event, relationship, and circumstance have the potential to grow into something magnificent. It is often accompanied by periods of pain but through remembrance and mourning, trauma does not hold us captive. Whatever writing process you decide to practice, just get it done. Don't sit around and think about it, sit down, and write. I hope this book and your writing practice continue to bring you hope and healing.

References

Brewin, C. R. & Lennard, H. (1999). Effects of mode of writing on emotional narratives. *Journal of Traumatic Stress, 12*, 355-361.

Cameron, J. (2020). *The artist's way: A spiritual path to higher creativity.* Souvenir Press. Great Britain.

Cameron, J. (2014). *The creative life: True tales of inspiration.* Audible Studios.

Cronin, E., Brand, B. L., & Mattanah, J. F. (2014). The impact of the therapeutic alliance on treatment outcome in patients with dissociative disorders. *European Journal of Psychotraumatology, 5.*

Duchin, A. & Wiseman, H. (2019). Memoirs of child survivors of the Holocaust: Processing and healing of trauma through healing. *Society for Qualitative Inquiry in Psychology, 6*(3), 280-296.

Goldberg, N. (2011). *The art of writing memoir: Finding the past in the present.* Writer's AudioShop.

Goldberg, N. (2008). *Writing down the bones.* Sounds True.

Karr, M. (2015). *The art of memoir.* HarperAudio.

Loewenstein, R. J. (2018). Dissociation debates: everything you know is wrong. *Dialogues in Clinical Neuroscience, 20*(3), 229-242.

Lucero, I. (2018). Written in the body? Healing the epigenetic molecular wounds of complex trauma through empathy and kindness. *Journal of Child & Adolescent Trauma, 11*, 443-455.

Maroney, D. I. (2020). The Imagine Project: Using expressive writing to help children overcome stress and trauma. *Continuing Nursing Education, 46*(6).

Pennebaker, J. W. & Smyth, J. M. (2016). *Opening up by writing it down.* The Guilford Press. New York.

Pennebaker, J.W. (2013). *Writing to heal. A guided journal for recovering from trauma & emotional upheaval.* Center for Journal Therapy. Wheat Ridge, CO.

Perryman, K., Blisard, P., & Moss, R. (2019). Using creative arts in trauma therapy: The neuroscience of healing. *Journal of Mental Health Counseling, 41*(1), 80-94.

Siegel, D. J. (2011). *The neurobiology of 'We.'* Sounds True.

Van der kolk, B. A. (2003). The neurobiology of childhood trauma and abuse. *Child Adolesc Psychiatric Clin N Am, 12*, 293-317.

Waite, R. & Ryan, R. A. (2020). *Adverse childhood experiences. What students and health professionals need to know.* Routledge. New York, NY.

www.ingramcontent.com/pod-product-compliance
Lightning Source LLC
Chambersburg PA
CBHW072152100526
44589CB00015B/2197